CHRONICLES OF LONG KESH

Martin Lynch

CHRONICLES OF LONG KESH

OBERON BOOKS
LONDON

First published in 2010 by Oberon Books Ltd
521 Caledonian Road, London N7 9RH
Tel: 020 7607 3637 / Fax: 020 7607 3629
e-mail: info@oberonbooks.com
www.oberonbooks.com

Reprinted in 2011

A catalogue record for this book is available from the British
Library.

PB ISBN: 978-1-84943-000-5
E ISBN: 978-1-84943-752-3

Cover design by three creative co. ltd.

Chronicles of Long Kesh received its World Premiere in Belfast, in January 2009, at the Waterfront Hall Studio. It was produced by Green Shoot Productions.

The play was directed by Lisa May and Martin Lynch. The original cast was as follows:

FREDDIE	Billy Clarke
EAMONN & OTHERS	Chris Corrigan
THUMPER & OTHERS	Laine Megaw
OSCAR & OTHERS	Marty Maguire
HANK & OTHERS	Andy Moore
TOOT & OTHERS	Marc O'Shea
Set & Costume Design	David Craig
Lighting Design	Conleth White
Musical Director	Paul Boyd
Fight Director	Paul Burke

The action of the play is set in Northern Ireland's infamous prison, Long Kesh/The Maze between 1971 - 2000

ACT 1

Off-stage we hear military marching orders being shouted out, to the sound of feet banging in unison.

VOICE: Company! Attennnn – shun! Companyyyyy, by the lefttttt, quick march!

Two single lines of marching men enter from opposite sides of the stage to join up and form a unit of six at centre-stage. Although dressed in casual civilian clothes, i.e. jeans and T-shirts, they have a military bearing and march well together.

VOICE: Company, halt! Stand at ease! Atten – shun! Right turn! Right turn! About turn! Companyyyy, by the leftttt, quick mark!

They march downstage, briefly marching on the spot when they reach the apron edge.

VOICE: Companyyyyy – wheel!

The marchers break off and take up various roles.

A couple of FARMERS are working with pitch forks. They stop as the noise of a WORKMAN using a pneumatic drill overwhelms them. The drill noise eases. They peer into the distance.

FARMER 1: Hey, What the hell's all thon yonder about then?

FARMER 2: Somebody workin' at the old RAF aerodrome.

FREDDIE enters. He is a man in his 50's, a Prison Officer, genial, gentle and with an easy-going manner.

FREDDIE: Little were these farmers to know it would be a new prison camp. Soon to become famous the world over as Long Kesh.

FARMER 1: Probably more bloody houses to spoil the countryside!

FREDDIE: I read up and discovered that it took its name from the Irish for the lush farmland of the Lagan – ceis fada – the long meadow.

FARMER 2: Sure y'never know. We could end up with a bunch of lovely new neighbours.

FREDDIE: Oh. My name's Freddie Gillespie. Apart from a deep love of Everton Football Club – I honestly had no idea I would end up a Prison Officer and that that pneumatic drill would draw me to its rattle, like a child to a fairground – some fairground.

The marchers resume their marching and fall into formation again at centre-stage.

VOICE: Company! Atten – shun! Stand at ease! Atten – shun!

OSCAR steps forward from the formation as though he was going to speak but breaks into song instead.

He sings one line from 'The Tracks Of My Tears'.

Oscar steps back into the formation and they do 3 seconds more of drilling. They stop and EAMON steps forward.

He sings a line from 'All My Loving' by the Beatles.

More brief drilling. HANK steps forward.

He sings a line from 'A Hard Rain's a-Gonna Fall' by Bob Dylan

More brief drilling. TOOT steps forward. He does a tasty wee dance as he sings.

He sings a line from 'Sugar, Sugar' as recorded by The Archies. This makes the others laugh.

More brief drilling. THUMPER steps forward. His singing is angry.

Thumper sings a line from 'You Really Got Me' by The Kinks.

More brief drilling.

OSCAR: Companyyyy, halt! Atten – shun! Right turn! By the left, quick march!

They march to the edge of stage-right where they briefly mark time.

OSCAR: Companyyyy, halt!

They immediately break ranks and adopt roles.

EAMON Jennings is pointing at a blackboard in class.

EAMON: Everybody got that? Always – always – double check – treble check – the sealings on an S bend, saves potential problems down the road.

FREDDIE: Eamon Jennings. Plumber by trade, part-time night-class teacher. The year is 1971 and Eamon is also an Auxiliary in the Provisional Irish Republican Army.

EAMON: *(To class.)* Any questions?

FREDDIE: Not a fully fledged member of the IRA, but a reserve for the main body. Eamon came in very useful when the IRA needed to hide its guns.

EAMON and another auxiliary, TOOT are at work constructing a hide in the living room of a house. TOOT has been hammering a chisel into a brick wall for some time. Being a Beatles fan, EAMON is happily dinging a line from his favourite beatles song.

TOOT: Is that it?

FREDDIE: Anthony 'Toot' McGinley, another recent recruit to the Auxiliaries. Toot wasn't the sharpest tack in the box, but he wanted to do his bit for Ireland.

EAMON: Ok, we've taken away the iron breastplate at the back of the fire, knocked away the wall behind it...

TOOT: I knocked away the wall behind it.

EAMON: Toot knocked the wall away – and before you know it, we have a big enough space to put half a dozen rifles.

TOOT: Re-plaster and repaint...

EAMON: ...and bob's your-uncle.

TOOT: You're a smart man, Eamon.

They have a congratulatory handshake.

FREDDIE: Eamon Jennings was an angry young man.

TOOT: Why did you get involved, Eamon?

EAMON: Because something has to be done. Catholics don't have a chance in this place. Never did. Go and have a look at my Da. A decent man, welder by trade. Spent the best of his workin' life unemployed. Scared to speak up. Catholics didn't speak up in those days. Shuffles about now, from the pub to the bookies. On the scrap heap at 50. Our people have been made to eat shit as second-class citizens – in their own country. Enough's enough. It's fight-back time.

FREDDIE: My uncle was a Breadman. By the time I was nineteen I was getting up at four o clock in the mornin' and doin my own delivery round, all over Ballynafeigh.

FREDDIE addresses a woman.

Right missus.

The WOMAN is an old battleaxe with a raspy, smokers cough.

WOMAN: Two pan loaves, four sodas and three currant squares.

FREDDIE: No problem.

(To audience.) Whilst I was at the Bread, a young lad called Hank was beginnin' his apprenticeship in the Shipyard.

HANK enters with a FOREMAN. HANK is a pained teenager, struggling with fitting into conventional life, is veering towards hippyism.

FOREMAN: What's the name?

HANK: Hank. *(The foreman looks at him quizzically.)* I don't have a second name anymore. I'm tryin' to...find myself at the moment, y'know?

FREDDIE: William Alexander McNeely or Hank to his friends. In 1971 Hank was a buddin' hippie. Long hair, Bob Dylan fan, smokin' plenty of weed.

HANK: I'm very interested in travellin' to India, y'know. Wanna check out this Transcendental meditation shit.

FOREMAN: Right. You're workin' in the Weldin' shop til we get a reference from the Marharishi Yogi, Ok?

FREDDIE: When I was 21 a got married and it wasn't long before the first child came along. Money was tight. I remember lookin' at the Jobs section in the *Belfast Telegraph* and there were these two big advertisements, side by side: The Police and The Prison Service. The money sounded great. Then it came on the news.

NEWSREADER: Internment-without-trial has been introduced, leading to widespread rioting across the north. Hundreds of republicans have been taken into custody.

We hear the overwhelmingly loud noise of a helicopter, the roar of British Army Saracens and Pig Carriers, the banging of bin-lids, voices shouting, etc.

FREDDIE: The Catholic districts of Northern Ireland were up-in-arms.

EAMON Jennings is run onstage by two soldiers holding his arms behind his back. He is in his bare feet and shirtless. The soldiers violently pull his head by the hair, jerking it back repeatedly.

RESIDENT 1: Bastards! They've arrested men from Lurgan and Derry and all over the place!

RESIDENT 2: And that fella Eamon Jennings was taken out in his bare feet, no shirt nor nothin' on him!

FREDDIE: None of this affected us living in her Ma's house on the Cregagh Road. Except, we wanted a place of our own.

MAUREEN: I was down the Ravenhill Road lookin' at the wee house. It has it's own wee front garden and everything, it's lovely. Could we not buy it, Freddie?

FREDDIE: Every Friday I stared at those two advertisements.

EAMON is manhandled and beaten around a room by two excited soldiers, shouting questions and abuse as they do.

SOLDIER 1: What position do you hold in the IRA?

EAMON: I'm not in the IRA.

SOLDIER 2: You're a liar!

SOLDIER 1: Is David Campbell in the IRA?

EAMON: I don't know any David Campbell.

SOLDIER 1: Bastard

The soldiers lay into EAMON violently. They stop. EAMON is lying on the ground.

FREDDIE: At Crumlin Road Prison Eamon met the notorious Alex Spencer, a Prison Officer.

SPENCER: Confirm your name please?

EAMON: Eamon Jennings.

SPENCER: Eamon? That's a fenian name, isn't it?

EAMON is roughly escorted away.

FREDDIE: I was still staring at those advertisements in the Belfast Telegraph. I didn't know what to do for the best. Then...

MAUREEN: We're havin' another baby.

FREDDIE: Holy shit. *(To audience.)* Since I couldn't decide between the Police or the Prison Service – you won't believe this – I tossed a coin. True. I'll never forget my first day in Crumlin Road Jail.

Two Prison Officers, FREDDIE and STEAL THE SHEETS (STS) walk along a wing.

FREDDIE: Archie McTaggart, otherwise known as Steal The Sheets. From Glasgow originally, but now married to an Armagh woman.

STS stops, checks with his watch and fills in a form. FREDDIE feels very awkward in his new Prison Uniform. He keeps checking his hat, his shirt and tie and his prison baton to make sure they are positioned properly. STEAL THE SHEETS is a very nervy type, He speaks out the side of his mouth in machine-gun like snatches. Always surreptitiously smoking a cigarette and blowing the smoke out the side of his mouth.

STEAL THE SHEETS: Where you fa, kid?

FREDDIE: Archie used to work in the Women's prison in Armagh. His favourite trick was to steal bed linen from the laundry and gettin' his brother-in-law to sell it at Jonesboro Market.

STS: When did y'say y'started?

FREDDIE: Just Monday there.

STS: Well, for Jesus sake watch yourself. There's some bad boys in here nigh. Gone are the days of your oul decent purse thief.

FREDDIE: So I hear.

STS: And watch out for the messers. They see a red band on the wings, they know you're on probation and they'll try and take ye for a ride. Don't let the fuckers away with nothin', ok? See you later.

STEAL THE SHEETS turns and locks FREDDIE on the other side of the gate and begins to walk away. FREDDIE is shocked.

FREDDIE: Here? Here, where you goin'?

STS: Back to duty on C Wing.

FREDDIE: You've just locked me in.

STS: And?

FREDDIE: What a shock! I thought it was supposed to be me doin' the lockin' up.

A Prisoner, TOOT appears.

TOOT: Excuse me, mate.

FREDDIE: What's that?

TOOT: Just lettin' you know I'm the Provisional IRA OC round here. You have to do what I tell ye.

FREDDIE: What's your name?

TOOT: Toot McGinley.

FREDDIE: You remember Toot? He might not have been the full shillin' but he had a certain craftiness.

TOOT: Only messing about. I'm not the Provo OC, I'm an innocent man. I shouldn't be here. Everybody knows I'm not in the IRA. Here, can you get me a real knife and fork?

FREDDIE: Internment was by now, in full swing, shootin's, bombin's, assassinations and riots were the order of the day. Something happened to laid-back Hank the young Shipyard worker that changed who he was.

We hear an explosion, the blaring of police and ambulance sirens. A MAN staggers backwards across stage banging into HANK, his hands covered in blood. HANK tries to grab the man and talk to him but without success.

MAN: Jesis Christ! Where's the fuckin Peelers. Jesis Christ!

HANK: What's the story man, what the fuck's happened?

FREDDIE: One of the early IRA bombs was in a furniture store on the Shankill Road – a six-month old baby was killed as she lay in her pram.

The MAN turns around and around, appealing in desperation.

MAN: Can nobody do nothin'!

A Stern-looking UVF MAN is standing drinking in a pub. HANK approaches him.

HANK: Your name Kelly?

UVF MAN: Who's askin'?

HANK: My name's Hank.

UVF MAN: What's your problem, Hank?

HANK: I wanna join the Protestant Volunteer Force.

FREDDIE: I was now able to put the deposit down for the wee house on the Ravenhill Road – garden and all – and – buy a second hand Hillman Imp for £250.

MAUREEN: Next week we'll get the whole house painted, then we'll get carpets for all the bedrooms. Oh Freddie, I am so excited.

FREDDIE: Hold on a minute Maureen love, I'm only a rookie Prison Officer, not Nelson Rockafella.

MAUREEN: Never worry. *(She kisses him affectionately.)* By the way. I'd like us to get a phone in, please.

FREDDIE: Okay, darlin'.

(To audience.) I was settling in rightly at work. Republicans were coming in in hordes. They were rough, tough, angry, even arrogant. Their command structure was very efficient and nobody messed them about.

FREDDIE: Alright lads, into the canteen.

The men don't move. They stare back at FREDDIE. Eventually EAMON approaches FREDDIE.

EAMON: We're members of the Irish Republican Army. We'll go into the canteen when we want to go into the canteen. OK!

EAMON moves right up to FREDDIE's face and stares him out before blowing air in his face, EAMON turns and nods for the others who laugh as they join him in the canteen.

FREDDIE: There were a few odd balls too – like Dominic Donnelly.

DOMINIC DONNELLY enters the canteen. He has a long face, never smiles, is permanently depressed and usually complaining from some illness or other. He seems to relish passing on bad news about other peoples illnesses, deaths, etc.

DOMINIC: Any of yousens any painkillers?

EAMON: What's wrong, Dominic?

DOMINIC: A think a'm gettin' rheumatoid arthritis. Pain's terrible.

EAMON: Haven't got any. I could lend you a few books, take your mind off things.

DOMINIC: Books! Are you away in the fuckin' head?

EAMON: I've just finished a good one called Candide. It's all about a guy who travels the world and all he concludes that the world is a terrible place.

DOMINIC: You tryin' to wind me up?

EAMON: No, I just think you'd get a lot out of it.

DOMINIC: Fuck books. All books are shite. *(Moves to exit and then stops.)* Oh, did yiz hear? Twenty of our lads caught at a Gun Lecture in Andytown. They'll be comin' in any minute. Stupid cunts.

No painkillers, then?

The men shake their heads. DOMINIC walks off disgusted. Speaks under his breath.

Fuckin' books.

EAMON: It's mad, isn't it? I was lyin' in bed last night thinkin', 'Six weeks ago life was normal. I was a plumber with a wife and two kids. Here I am in Jail.' Weird or what?

TOOT: What did I do? Knocked down the back wall of an oul doll's fireplace and here I am bein' treated as if I'm Michael fuckin' Collins.

At this, OSCAR enters. OSCAR is loud, lively, jolly, coarse and reckless. He is a prowler, restless, always moving about, seldom sits for very long. He is carrying a bag, has a newspaper, magazines, etc. He shouts loudly for all to hear.

OSCAR: Okay, what's for dinner, hey? There better be no shite onions in it!

FREDDIE: Oliver 'Oscar' Coyle. From Londonderry.

OSCAR: Any Derry men in here?

The men shake their heads slowly.

Fucksake, this is gonna be good. Am I goin' to have to live among a crowd of ball-less Belfast wans.

TOOT: There's a guy in from Strabane.

OSCAR: Fuck Strabane, they're all arseholes.

FREDDIE: Oscar is a quartermaster in the IRA Derry Brigade.

EAMON: Where'd y'get all the newspapers and magazines?

OSCAR: What are you? A fuckin' peeler?

EAMON: Only askin'.

OSCAR: Only jokin' ya, big lad. A wee guy down in the basement gave me them for a few fegs.

Holds them up.

Not bad, eh? 'Nude girls from Bradford.' 'Faye Dunaway, full nude shots. Fuckin' great, what? And this is supposed to be jail

He roars laughing.

Have d'hurry up and get this dinner into me and get away for a good wank.

Roars laughing again, slapping his thigh.

FREDDIE: It wasn't long before Loyalists began to react to the renewed IRA campaign of violence. Hank the would-be hippy was now Hank the willing but footless UVF man.

A UVF OFFICER marches onstage, followed by HANK and THUMPER marching behind. THUMPER is a very sharp dresser, continuously checking and rechecking his clothes, hair, shoes, etc. He is lean and fit and can take care of himself.

UVF OFFICER: Left, right, left, right. Companyyyyy halt!

They halt in unison.

Companyyyyy stand at ease!

Ok, Thumper, give Hank a run down on the operation. Transport'll be here shortly.

The Officer exits. HANK is exhausted. He lets out a sound of exasperated pain.

HANK: Why didn't I go to San Franciso when I had the chance?

THUMPER: As long as your good at whackin' fenians, that's all that matters.

FREDDIE: Billy Thumper McKibben. A tasty-dressin' UVF man.

THUMPER: Right, it's a pub near the New Lodge. The Provos are usin' upstairs for meetin's.

FREDDIE: Believe it or not Thumper had O levels. He wore a shirt and tie to the office every day at a big Timber Yard down the docks.

HANK: You wearin' that suit?

THUMPER: What's it to you? This – is tailor-made, outta Burtons.

HANK: Only askin'. Chill man. *(Beat.)* So, we're gonna hit this meetin'?

THUMPER: No, fuck that. We're gonna plant a big bomb in the downstairs bar and riddle the fuck outiv anybody we see.

HANK: Anybody? Is that...cool?

THUMPER: Cool? Where the fuck did the get you? Listen, mate. These bastards are attackin' our country. Everything your Da, your granda, your great granda, built this country up to be is under threat right now. What does any decent man do when his country is bein' attacked?

HANK: Fights back.

THUMPER: Right, that's better. Here, where'd you get that shirt? It's not a Ben Sherman, is it?

THUMPER goes to the back of HANK and begins, roughly, trying to find the label on the inside of Hank's shirt. The UVF OFFICER re-enters.

UVF OFFICER: Okay, transport's here. Let's go!

The men immediately jump to attention. We hear a loud explosion accompanied by a blackout, gunfire, a split-second flash of light, followed by smoke. HANK and THUMPER are lying on the ground. HANK stumbles to his feet. He takes in the scene.

HANK: Thumper! *(Beat.)* Thumper, you ok?

THUMPER: Yeah, I'm okay. But m'fuckin' good suit's ruined.

HANK goes over and helps him to his feet. They stumble off.

FREDDIE: Somehow, Hank and Thumper managed to escape with a fairly light sentence. Inside, the loyalists were just as tough and arrogant as the republicans.

HANK and THUMPER approach FREDDIE.

THUMPER: Hey yo! Over here a minute.

FREDDIE: My name's not Yo. I'm Officer Gillespie to you.

THUMPER: Yeah, yeah. Listen, we have something we need help with.

FREDDIE: Like what?

THUMPER: I need a white shirt and some Levi jeans in. My Granny can bring them up in a visit.

FREDDIE: Sorry, not allowed.

THUMPER: Hank.

HANK: Wife's name is Maureen. She works part-time in a Bakery on the Woodstock Road. Has one child Alan and another on the way. Maureen gets the bus home every day at a quarter to five at the bus stop directly facin' the Bakery.

Freddie is initially shocked. Overcoming this, he resigns himself.

HANK: Here. My sister will be up with a guitar...and m'Bob Dylan LP, ok?

FREDDIE storms off. HANK and THUMPER burst into laughter. They start clowning. They sing a line from 'You Really Got Me' by The Kinks.

FREDDIE: My first experience of bein' knobbled. I had to step up my security.

MAUREEN: No.

FREDDIE: Look, I'll get financial support from the Service to help me with the move. We'll end up in a bigger, better house.

MAUREEN: No.

FREDDIE: Maureen, we have to move house for security reasons.

MAUREEN: Well...maybe we have to, but I'm not goin' round tellin' the neighbours you work as a chef.

FREDDIE: It's security.

MAUREEN: The house has to be near my mother's.

FREDDIE: We moved to a semi-detached on the other side of the Knock Dual carriageway. Maureen loved it. *(Beat.)* On the Prison front, I didn't know I was about to walk into a Tamla Motown hit factory.

FREDDIE approaches a cell occupied by EAMON, OSCAR and TOOT. OSCAR is rehearsing TOOT to sing harmony on a song, 'Reach Out, I'll Be There'. They sing together really well. As they start the song they slip into a well-rehearsed dance routine and are quickly joined by EAMON.

When the soul song is over the others stop singing but TOOT carries on, whipping off his shirt, doing a mad attempt at a sexy, dance routine.

TOOT: *(He suddenly realises the others aren't singing with him.)* Ah, fucksake...

OSCAR: Toot we are not doing that. And you are a tuneless fucker. Smokey Robinson would be ashamed if he heard you.

TOOT: There's nothing wrong with my singin'.

OSCAR: Eamon, you have a go?

EAMON: Not a hope.

OSCAR: We need to have this song ready for the Christmas concert.

Freddie enters.

FREDDIE: Sorry to be such a spoil sport lads, but the next concert you'll be at will be in Long Kesh.

We hear the momentary loud noise of a helicopter. Carrying their bags, EAMON, OSCAR and TOOT enter a hut in Long Kesh.

TOOT: That helicopter was beezer, wasn't it?

OSCAR: Pity we couldn't hijack it.

EAMON: Long Kesh by-the-sea.

OSCAR: It would remind you of Butlins. Without the sexy redcoats.

TOOT: I like it.

EAMON: What?

OSCAR: What is there to like?

TOOT: I mean, it's spacey.

OSCAR: You're fuckin' spacey.

EAMON: You wait Toot, til you're tryin' to get a sleep at night with 50 or 60 people in the same room crawling and fartin' and snorin' all over the place.

TOOT: How long do you think we"ll be here, Oscar?

OSCAR: How do I know? I'm not the Jail Govenor. But I did hear somebody mentioning 12 years.

TOOT: 12 years! No way. All I did was knock down an oul doll's fireplace and they're gonna lock me up for twelve years! I'm not even in the IRA.

OSCAR: We'll just have to escape.

EAMON: Some chance.

OSCAR: What, sure it's only nissen huts and barbed wire. I'll be sinkin' pints into me in The Sunbeam Bar by Christmas.

EAMON: Dream on.

OSCAR: You watch. *(Beat.)* I'm takin' this bed.

TOOT: I'll take the one beside you, Oscar.

OSCAR flops on a bed.

OSCAR: Fuck away aff. You're not sleepin' beside me, y'smelly cunt.

EAMON: Toot you take that one and I'll take this one beside ye. *(Beat.)* Right, better check out the bogs.

EAMON exits.

TOOT: Hey, look at the seagulls. Tons of them, there is.

OSCAR: Noisy bastards they are too.

TOOT: What are they doin' here?

OSCAR: They're deliberately put there by the Brits, to remind us we're in jail.

TOOT: Look at the size of them.

STEAL THE SHEETS enters. OSCAR and TOOT go over and stand beside him.

STS: Mail for Hut 4!

OSCAR: Holy fuck, look who it is? Steal The Sheets himself.

TOOT: The Prison Service's answer to Ronnie Biggs.

OSCAR: How does a thief get a job guarding decent honourable men?

STS: Mail transferred from the Crum.

(Reads names on letters.)

McGinley!

TOOT: For me? *(TOOT snatches his letter.)*

STS: Coyle!

OSCAR: That's me! *(OSCAR snatches his letter.)*

STS: O'Neill, Jennings...

TOOT: I'll take that for Eamon.

TOOT fetches Eamon's letter.

STS: That's the lot. Yous lads all settlin' in, okay?

OSCAR: Fuck off, y'Scotch mercenary bastard!

STEAL THE SHEETS exits. OSCAR is reading his letter.

TOOT: Who's the letter from?

OSCAR: M'wife, Briege. She says the baby's due in 3 weeks. She says she's callin' it Damian. *(Beat.)* Who the fuck's Damian?

TOOT: Are you sure there's no Damian in the family?

OSCAR: No. *(Beat.)* Oh, hold on. Her Da's called Damian. Forgot about him.

EAMON enters.

TOOT: Letter for ya Eamon.

EAMON: Thanks.

OSCAR: Who's yours from Toot?

TOOT hands EAMON his letter.

TOOT: Who's it from, Eamon?

EAMON: It's from...Thomas.

OSCAR: Who's Thomas?

TOOT: Just a mate lives across the street from me. Would you read it for me Eamon, please?

OSCAR: Here, listen to this. Briege says, 'I asked your father if he wanted me to put his name down for a visit with you and he says 'hell will freeze over first'. He says 'your job has gone and he never wants to set eyes on you again,'

OSCAR roars with laughter.

Oul bastard. You can shove your job up your arse, Jimmy 'Mister Respectable' Coyle!

TOOT: What job, what job is he talkin' about?

OSCAR: The feckin undertakin' shite.

TOOT: You an undertaker?

OSCAR: My Da runs an undertakin' business and he had me doin' it, the crazy bastard.

TOOT: Did ya not like dealin' with dead bodies?

OSCAR: No, dead bodies were a doddle. It was my Da I couldn't stand. I blame him. If I hadna had the use of the hearse I wouldn'ta ended up smugglin' guns across the border, would a?

TOOT: It wasn't your Daddy made y'smuggle the guns.

OSCAR: Shut the fuck up, you and your alcoholic Ma.

TOOT: My Ma's not an alcoholic.

OSCAR: She is.

TOOT: She isn't.

OSCAR: She is.

Annoyed, TOOT speaks under his breath as he turns away to lie down.

TOOT: Fuck off, Oscar.

Silence. The three men read their letters.

OSCAR: What's wrong with you Jennings, you're very quiet?

EAMON: Nothin'.

OSCAR: Everything alright?

EAMON: More or less.

OSCAR: The wife hasn't fucked off and left ya?

EAMON: No. I just feel so guilty.

OSCAR: I don't. I wished I hada killed every Brit I ever set eyes on.

EAMON: I'm not talkin' about that. I'm talkin' about m'wife. The kids. I have done a terrible thing to them.

OSCAR: Ack, we'll be outta here in no time. Stick with me Jennings and I'll have ye over that wire before Christmas.

EAMON: I couldn't care less about escapin' I'm more concerned about how I'm ever gonna pay back my wife.

OSCAR: Shite. The women and childer can wait. We have to get the Brits outta Ireland first. *(Beat.)* What's the bogs like?

EAMON: Basic, but they'll do.

OSCAR: Right. Nothin' else for it. I'm away for a rub of the relic.

OSCAR exits. Silence.

TOOT: Eamon?

EAMON: Yeah.

TOOT: Would you write a letter out to my Ma?

EAMON: Yes, but better still, startin' tomorrow I'm gonna teach you how to read and write, ok?

TOOT: Y'can't teach me, Eamon. All my teachers think I'm a dunce.

EAMON: Let me decide that. Good night.

Silence.

TOOT: Eamon?

EAMON: What Toots?

TOOT: I kinda...like it in here.

EAMON: Do ya?

TOOT: Yeah. It's...it's better, like...it's better than our house with my Ma's on the sauce.

EAMON: Let's get some sleep, Toot.

Silence.

TOOT: Eamon?

EAMON: What, Toot?

TOOT: I have a meetin' with my solicitor tomorrow.

EAMON: What for?

TOOT: D'get me outta here, whadaya think. I'm innocent, remember.

EAMON: Who's your solicitor?

TOOT: Nigel McKee.

EAMON roars laughing.

You know him?

EAMON: Everybody knows Nigel 'moneybags' McKee.

NIGEL MCKEE, solicitor arrives.

FREDDIE: Nigel McKee. He has dozens of prisoners to see and wanting to rake in as much cash as possible he crams them all in to half an hour.

TOOT: is sitting at a table. Nigel enters, flustered, opening his briefcase and smoking a cigarette at the same time. He points at Toot.

NIGEL: Bradley, double murder?

TOOT: No, McGinley, going to the Internee court.

NIGEL: That's right. McGinley, going to the Internee court. You're from Lurgan?

TOOT: No, Belfast.

NIGEL: Belfast. Sorry about that Patrick.

TOOT: Anthony.

NIGEL: *(Quickly.)* Anthony.

FREDDIE: Whilst the Republicans were getting to know Long Kesh and each other, yards away the Loyalists were doin' exactly the same.

In the UVF Compound, The OFFICER enters. He starts banging the beds with an iron bar, creating a loud racket.

OFFICER: Okay, okay, rise and shine! It's January the first, 1972. Happy new year everybody! C'mon. Outta your beds and on your feet.

The men groan and complain.

THUMPER: Fucksake.

THUMPER and HANK get up and sit on the edge of their beds. They are groggy.

Suddenly, THUMPER throws himself to the floor and begins a series of physical exercises.

HANK: Jesis. Every morning, twice durin' the day and last thing at night. You dig all this keep-fit shit, man?

THUMPER: It's habit. M'Da was a body builder. He was always workin' out too.

HANK: Does he still do it?

THUMPER: Don't know. Left when I was 15. Moved to Doncaster in England with his fancy woman.

HANK: Must be hard for your mother.

THUMPER: She fucked off too. I live with m'granny. My granny is my Ma. And m'Da.

THUMPER stands up.

You got my shampoo?

HANK: I lent it to Nosebleed.

THUMPER is suddenly seething with anger.

THUMPER: What?

FREDDIE: There's no place like prison to see men behavin' at their worst. I have seen blood spilt over roast potatoes.

HANK: He said he'd bring it back.

THUMPER: You owe me a full bottle of Citrus Fruit Vosene shampoo!

HANK: Well what happened about you getting me in my Bob Dylan LP

THUMPER: Who wants to listen to that cunt.

HANK: *(Getting serious.)* Hit it in the head, Thumper. Bob Dylan is a genuine creative artiste.

FREDDIE: Add Bob Dylan to the roast potatoes and the shampoo and you have a typical day in Long Kesh. *(Beat.)* If you believe that's all went on, you'd believe anything.

In the Republican Compound, OSCAR is holding an imitation Sterling sub-machine gun. EAMON and TOOT are paying rapt attention.

OSCAR: This is a Sterling sub machine gun. Fires 9 millimetre rounds at the rate of approximately 500 per minute. It's accurate up to a hundred yards with the single shot.

TOOT: Could you repeat that?

OSCAR: It's accurate up to a hundred yards with a single shot.

TOOT: No, the bit before.

OSCAR: For fucksake, will y'pay attention Toot? It fires 9 millimetre rounds at the rate of 500 per minute?

TOOT: Yes, that bit. That's ferocious, isn't it.

OSCAR: It weighs 2.72 kilos, pretty light and manageable – compared to say, the Thompson. The weapon is constructed entirely of steel and plastic and has a folding butt which folds up underneath, like so.

TOOT: That's clever. That's clever, isn't it Eamon?

OSCAR: Toot, fuck up! Although it's of conventional blowback design, there are some unusual features: for example...

TOOT: If yiz can make imitations as good as that, why don't yiz make real ones?

OSCAR: Holy fuck. *(Exasperated.)* Okay, that's it. Companyyyyyy! Attentionnnnn!

EAMON and TOOT immediately stand to attention. TOOT is a bit footless and awkward.

Stand at ease!

Fall out. Eamon I wanna word with you.

They distance themselves from TOOT.

OSCAR: I want you to help the Escape Committee.

EAMON nods.

Are y'game?

EAMON: No problem. Anything.

OSCAR: As soon as I know what the story is, I'll give you a shout, ok?

EAMON: I'm your man.

OSCAR: Good. Now, can y'be in the half hut at eight a clock sharp?

EAMON: Yes.

OSCAR: Sound. I want you to work on a couple of Smokey songs with me for the concert.

EAMON: What?

OSCAR: The Cage concert.

EAMON: I don't know any Smokey Robinson songs? I know plenty of Beatles songs.

OSCAR: How can anybody go through life without knowin' any Smokey Robinson songs? That's like never tastin' a fried egg on potato farl. Do y'know, 'My Guy'?

EAMON: How does it go?

Oscar sings a line from the song.

Know it?

EAMON: Aye but that's a woman's song

OSCAR: Yes, but Smokey wrote it. Great. Eight a clock tonight in the half hut.

OSCAR sings cheerily as he walks away.

FREDDIE enters.

FREDDIE: Visit for Coyle!

OSCAR: That's me!

He sings another line from 'My Guy'. The others join in the singing.

OSCAR stands up. He spits on his hands and flatten his hair. He jerks his shoulders a couple of times to psyche himself up, then walks off with FREDDIE. They arrive at the visiting area. His wife, BRIEGE is waiting. FREDDIE stands guard. OSCAR stops and feints. He points at BRIEGE in a large gesture and shouts across the room.

OSCAR: Hey! Are you madly in love with me or what?

BRIEGE: Wise up, you.

OSCAR: *(Loudly.)* I love my wife!

They hug and kiss then sit down.

Well, how goes it?

BRIEGE: Great. Everything's goin' fine. I know y'wanted me to bring Damian up but I thought it would be too much for him.

OSCAR: Definitely next time.

BRIEGE: I was talkin' to your Daddy on Tuesday.

OSCAR: What were y'talkin to that bollicks for?

BRIEGE: He rang me to tell me there was two weeks holiday pay belongin' to you sittin' in the office.

OSCAR: Did y'get it?

BRIEGE: Got the child a new pram and two sets of clothin' and I'm tryin' to hold on to the rest of it to see me through.

OSCAR: Good, good. After this, have no contact with him whatsoever, y'hear me?

BRIEGE: It's not exactly how I thought m'life would pan out but it's okay.

OSCAR: Y'getting' out?

BRIEGE: I go to the pub with our Eileen and her boyfriend Owen most Friday nights. But I only have a few vodkas and I'm back in m'bed and reading Victoria Holt before twelve a clock.

OSCAR: Y'sure?

BRIEGE: Whadaya mean, am a sure?

OSCAR: Isn't there dancin' in the pub on Friday night?

BRIEGE: Yes.

OSCAR: And?

BRIEGE: I did dance with Owen one night but that's about it.

OSCAR: You don't go out any other nights?

BRIEGE: No.

OSCAR: Definitely?

BRIEGE: Definitely.

OSCAR: Definitely, definitely, deffff-nitely?

BRIEGE: Oscar, I resent this. I'm a good wife to you. I look after the child – in your absence – with no man's wage comin' in. I send you up a parcel – a good parcel – every week.

OSCAR: Keep your voice down. *(Beat.)* I'm sorry.

BRIEGE: And so y'should be.

Silence.

OSCAR: *(Meekly.)* Any chance of a flash?

BRIEGE: What?

OSCAR: Any chance of a flash of your tits, g'on, Briege?

BRIEGE: Catch yourself on. Whadaya think I am?

OSCAR: Go on, please? Briege, I am a dedicated republican internee, incarcerated without trial for my beliefs, livin' on a starvation diet...surely I deserve a flash of a wife's tits?

BRIEGE is hesitant for a moment, then speaks emphatically.

BRIEGE: No. Definitely not. Now, give over. *(Beat.)* Is there any talk of yiz gettin' out?

OSCAR: I was gonna ask you that.

BRIEGE: Oh, the whole place is against internment. I was at a big march m'self last week, but...then people go back to doin' whatever they have to do. I don't. I have to rear a child and run a house without my husband and I resent it. *(Begins to weep.)* Oscar, sometimes I don't think I'm ever gonna get through. I look around that house and I don't have a penny to m'name. I don't know what's gonna

33

happen me and my chile, I just wanna scream. I just wanna scream my friggin' head off.

OSCAR: It's okay, Briege.

OSCAR gets up and puts his arms around BRIEGE. FREDDIE immediately reproaches him.

FREDDIE: Sorry, no contact between prisoners and...

OSCAR: Fuck off!

FREDDIE immediately stops. OSCAR stares at FREDDIE defiantly. FREDDIE hesitates, then backs off. OSCAR continues to console BRIEGE.

OSCAR: It'll be alright, Briege. Don't worry, we'll be out in no time...

Lights fade slowly on OSCAR and BRIEGE.

FREDDIE: Though I preferred bein' the one in the Prison Officer's uniform, when I had to do something like that, it made me think. When the prisoners wanted to think...

EAMON: Fancy a walk round the yard?

TOOT: C'mon.

EAMON and TOOT walk round and round the cage in silence. Other men walk around in small groups.

FREDDIE: Sometimes it was for exercise or just a yarn. Sometimes – like it was for Eamon right now – it was to fight off depression, the Big D.

EAMON: That's the thing, Toot – when you're sentenced, at least you have a release date. With Internment, we don't know shit.

TOOT: Hey look, there's the Official IRA prisoners getting released from Internment! *(Shouts.)* Go on y'cowardly bastards! Yiz hadn't got the guts d'fight the war!

OFFICIAL IRA MAN: It's better than bein' a bunch of stupid fuckers bein' led by a bunch of goats! See yiz in ten years!

TOOT: D'ya hear what he said? Ten years!

TOOT notices that EAMON isn't interested.

You alright, Eamon?

FREDDIE: While Eamon Jennings was struggling Toot had his own way of copin'.

TOOT is throwing bread to the seagulls.

TOOT: C'mon lads, you're not gonna tell me yiz aren't hungry. Look at yiz. Yous can fly to anywhere yiz like and whadaya do? Hang around a prison camp. Tell is this? How the fuck do y'fly?

EAMON stares back at TOOT, expressionless. DOMINIC enters. He is gripping a cloth snake belt tightly around his head with one hand at his forehead.

TOOT: Ah Dominic. What's with the belt wrapped round your head?

DOMINIC: Migraines. Get them every day.

TOOT: Can y'not get anything off the doctor?

DOMINIC: Aye. Two aspirin he gives me. No matter what's wrong with ye, all y'get in here is two fuckin' aspirin.

DOMINIC exits.

FREDDIE: The Prisoners hated the Prison doctors. Even though every day when we opened up the huts we had to offer them the services of a doctor.

STEAL THE SHEETS enters.

STS: Okay, who wants to see the doctor?

DOMINIC: Nobody wants d'see that fucker?

STS: Who called the doctor a fucker?

DOMINIC: Who called the fucker a doctor?

FREDDIE: As the Troubles intensified and Long Kesh began to resemble a sardine tin, the republicans began to speak Irish more and this gave Toot an idea.

TOOT and EAMON are talking.

TOOT: Look, y'have Londoners and Glaswegians – but Belfast has no equivalent description. But when you use the Irish word – Bealfeirste – we can call ourselves Bealfeirstians!

EAMON: Does have a ring about it.

TOOT: 'Toot McGinley was a Bealfeirstian who rose to great heights in his short life.'

FREDDIE: 1973 came and went, but 1974 was to be a very eventful year in the life of Long Kesh. Believe it or not, the biggest incident was over our old friend – food.

OSCAR: I don't give a toss. It's my job to check the food before it goes into the men. I counted the sausage rolls and there's only 82 – there's 86 men in here, that's four short.

FREDDIE: Oscar, I can only give out what's in that van.

Prison Officer, Alex SPENCER enters. He is a hard, tough bitter man who uses every opportunity he gets, to show how much he despises the prisoners.

SPENCER: What's goin' on here?

FREDDIE: PO Spencer, there seems to be a couple of sausage rolls short for this compound.

SPENCER: So.

OSCAR: So? We're not havin' it, Spencer.

SPENCER: Is that right? *(To Freddie.)* Officer Gillespie, drop this food off and get on with your duties.

FREDDIE: Yes, sir.

OSCAR: If that's the way yiz want it.

OSCAR turns to go.

SPENCER: Get back to whatever fenian hole you crawled out of, sonny boy.

OSCAR: OC! OC! Somebody get the OC out here. The screws are fuckin' about again!

We hear the roar of men charging, the sound of rubber bullets and CS Gas being fired, etc. We see prisoners attacking Prison officers and hand-to-hand combat ensuing. OSCAR, EAMON and TOOT enter in a hurry, exhausted, coughing and choking.

ALL: I! I! IRA! I! I! IRA!

FREDDIE: The next day, the British Army stormed the cages and took back control of the Prison. Not without a fight though. Maureen had been listenin' to the news.

MAUREEN: Well, I hear things on the news and I don't know if you're in the middle of it or if you're sittin' in the Club havin' a drink. I'm never told anything.

FREDDIE: I will ring you.

MAUREEN: Promise?

FREDDIE: I promise.

(To audience.) On a brighter note she was delighted when I was able to buy a new Morris Marina. Expensive, but my money – with overtime – was good now, and we were doin' well. In the prison, the end of 1974 brought great speculation about the ending of Internment.

TOOT: Two shillins, Internment is over by Christmas and Toot McGinley the Bealfeirstian will be back in the house eatin' a big fry.

FREDDIE: In the loyalist Compound, the lads were contemplatin' their own release.

HANK: Nine months and twenty eight days and I'll be shootin' back up that motorway.

THUMPER: Can't wait to get stuck into a big bowl of m'granny's stew.

HANK: As I was sayin, San Francisco, here I come.

THUMPER: If you ever make San Francisco, I'll be the next Pope. Now, my visit beckons. Susie Long Legs is waitin'. I wonder will she be wearin' any knickers? Whoopeeee!

THUMPER rubs his hands together in anticipation.

Now, after five mad years and all the Provos gettin' released, I wonder will they have the good sense to know they can't bomb the Prods into a United Ireland?

FREDDIE: The British Government announced Internment was ending. The internees were released in drips and drabs.

TOOT is pacing the floor carrying a black bag over his shoulders with one hand and a self-made large wooden Irish Harp with the other.

OSCAR: Will you, for christsake sit down!

TOOT: I'm waitin' on the names.

OSCAR: We're all waitin' on the names. But that bastard of a woman has just told me she's leavin' me to go and live in Wales. And takin' Damian with her. The last thing I want is you gettin' on m'nerves too.

TOOT: Sorry for breathin'. *(Beat.)* Hey Eamon, if your name's on the list you'll be hittin' the Club tonight, what?

EAMON: Naa Toot, I've done my whack. I won't be goin' back anywhere near the Club or the Republican Movement. I'm finito. And I certainly won't be back inside a prison ever again.

STEAL THE SHEETS enters.

TOOT: Here's Steal The Sheets with the names, lads!

The men gather round STEAL THE SHEETS excitedly.

STEAL THE SHEETS: Names for release today. All names read out should present themselves and their personal effects at 9.30 sharp at the compound gate. Gilmore, Sinclair, Larkin, Jennings...that's it.

STEAL THE SHEETS turns to go, then stops.

Oh, nearly forgot. One more. McGinley. Get your bags packed Toot son, and get the hell outta here.

There is restrained jubilation among the men, except for TOOT, who immediately does a couple of laps of honour, cheering and whooping.

FREDDIE: Before he left, Toot had to go and say goodbye to his beloved seagulls.

TOOT: If I was you I'd head off to Africa. I saw it on a documentary once. Amazin' place. Okay? See yiz, lads. Thanks for everything. Oh, and if yiz see Nelson Mandela, tell him I was askin' about him. He's a big, tall black fella.

FREDDIE: While Internment was comin' to an end poor Oscar was charged with an escape attempt and transferred to the sentenced cages.

OSCAR enters a new Compound with bag, etc.

DOMINIC: Ack Oscar, what about ye?

OSCAR: Ah fuck, no, not you Dominic.

DOMINIC: I better tell ye, there's a bad bout of diahorrea in this cage.

OSCAR: Right. Nothin' else for it. I'm away for a choke of the chicken.

FREDDIE: After the false dawn of peace in 1975, 1976 saw the Troubles back in full flow. The Prison was bursting at the seams. It was around this time things began to take a turn for me.

FREDDIE is slightly the worse for wear.

MAUREEN: Monday night.

FREDDIE: Yes, I called into the Club for a few before I came home.

MAUREEN: Tuesday afternoon.

FREDDIE: One drink. Now, I only had one drink on Tuesday.

MAUREEN: Thursday.

FREDDIE: Ah, big Noel the Scouser was leavin. A had d'go to his goin'-away Do.

MAUREEN: Aye, and your friends had to carry you in here out of the taxi.

FREDDIE: Maureen, you're exaggeratin'.

MAUREEN: I don't think I am. Freddie, the truth is you are drinkin' far too much these days.

FREDDIE: By now, I probably was spendin' too much time in the Prison Social Club. Among the prisoners, all the talk was about the building work goin' on in the prison.

OSCAR and DOMINIC are staring into the distance.

DOMINIC: Somebody said they're new administration offices but if they wanna give the prisoners what we really need – they'd build a Bookies, wouldn't the?

OSCAR: Dominic son. They're new prison blocks. *(Beat.)* Right nigh you, back to rehearsals.

DOMINIC attempts to leave.

Where do you think you're goin'?

DOMINIC: I have to get ready for a visit to the doctor. M'migraine's playin' up.

OSCAR: Never mind your migraines, we have d'get this song right for the OC's birthday 'Do'.

DOMINIC: I don't wanna do this.

OSCAR: C'mon, let's go. The full works, right?

OSCAR and DOMINIC sing a well-rehearsed/choreographed version of 'Tracks Of My Tears', where the singers act out the song, pointing to the tears roiling down their faces, etc.

Showing off, OSCAR hits an incredibly high note at the end and holds it forever.

DOMINIC: Oscar you fucking love yourself, don't ye!

FREDDIE: Eamon Jennings was out of prison eighteen months when...

EAMON is being interrogated by two Special Branch Policemen.

SB1: You're in Police custody Jennings. Start telling the truth. What time did you leave the house at?

EAMON: About half ten.

SB2: Where did you go?

EAMON: Down to John McGreevy's house.

SB1: Why?

EAMON: He had a motorbike for sale and I went down to have a look at it.

SB2: That's all?

EAMON: That's all.

SB1: You expect us to believe that?

EAMON: It's the truth.

SB2: And you know nothin' about the fact that an hour later, John McGreevy turned up in East Belfast along with three other gunmen and murdered two police officers?

EAMON: Absolutely nothin'.

SB1: Well, we have McGreevy in custody and he says you know a lot about it.

EAMON: He's a liar.

SB2: He says it was you supplied him with all the information about the movements of the two Police Officers and you handed him that information in his house at ten thirty that day, an hour before the operation.

EAMON: That's not true. I was down to see about buyin' a motorbike off him.

SB1: You're a liar!

EAMON: I wanna see my solicitor.

FREDDIE: Eamon was sentenced to double life – a recommended 25 years. His first visit with his wife was... painful.

EAMON is sitting across a table from his wife, CATHY. Throughout the visit, CATHY's approach is measured. She barely raises her voice. FREDDIE is standing guard nearby.

EAMON: You can't sell the house.

CATHY: What do you want me to do? I need the money. Who's gonna pay the mortgage?

EAMON: I'll work out something.

CATHY: I don't know how much it's worth now anyway. It's half wrecked. British Army raids made sure of that.

EAMON: I'll arrange for it to be repaired.

CATHY: No. I don't want to live in it on my own with two children for the next twenty five years.

EAMON: What does every other woman do?

CATHY: I don't care. And it's not you has to do it, it's me.

EAMON: The children will be too much for your mother at her age.

CATHY: She'll be okay.

Silence.

Why did you do this, Eamon?

EAMON: Please, Cathy.

CATHY: You swore to me. You swore on your children's lives you wouldn't get involved again.

EAMON: It wasn't what you think. Things just…just happened.

CATHY: Yeah. Just enough to get you a recommended 25 years.

EAMON: Look Cathy, there's nothin' I can do now to change what happened. But, please give me another chance.

CATHY: Why would a?

EAMON: Because I love you.

CATHY: Ha! You love me? Is this some kind of joke? You love me? *(Beat.)* You love me? Are you not getting' me mixed up with the Republican movement?

EAMON: You know I love you and the kids more than anything else in the world.

CATHY: Nooooo. No, Eamon Jennings. That's what you say. That's what you like to tell yourself. But your actions suggest something entirely different. Your actions suggest you love the Republican movement more than anything else in the world. Me and your children are way down the peckin' order, left-overs, stale buns. Isn't that right, Eamon?

EAMON shakes his bowed head.

Patrick is eight now. He'll be a man of thirty three when you get out.

EAMON begins to quietly weep.

Conan is six.

EAMON weeps audibly.

He'll be thirty one. You and I will be in our fifties.

CATHY stands up.

I have a lot of thinkin' to do.

CATHY walks to the exit and stops.

You goin' on this blanket protest?

EAMON doesn't answer. CATHY exits.

FREDDIE: When Internment was ended, so was the Special Category Status the prisoners had enjoyed since 1972. It meant they now had to conform to all prison regulations including the wearing of standard Prison uniforms.

FREDDIE hands OSCAR his new prison uniform.

FREDDIE: Coyle? Uniform.

OSCAR: You jokin', Gillespie?

FREDDIE: It's compulsory.

OSCAR: Shove it up your metropole.

FREDDIE: My place of work had now taken over from the Falls Road and South Armagh as the new frontline of the war.

EAMON Jennings is sharing a cell with OSCAR Coyle, his old internee friend. It is EAMON's first day on the Blanket protest.

OSCAR: Well, first day on the blanket, Jennings. How does it feel?

EAMON: Friggin' awful. This is it? Two mangey blankets and a mattress?

OSCAR: Wait a minute, you've got a plate and mug too.

EAMON: And a piss pot?

OSCAR: Don't forget your bible.

EAMON: Oscar, how have yous lived like this?

OSCAR: You get used to it.

EAMON: No way. I will never get used to this.

OSCAR: Twenty four hour lock-up as well. The only time you see the sun is when you go asleep at night and dream. And don't forget, every day you're on the protest, you get a day added on to your sentence.

EAMON: Holy mother sufferin' Jesis. How am I gonna stick this?

OSCAR: Don't worry. It's about to get worse. The Jail Leadership has taken a decision to step up the campaign.

EAMON: How?

OSCAR: A 'no-wash' protest.

EAMON: What does that mean?

OSCAR: What it says. We don't wash ourselves anymore. No washin', no shavin, no haircuts, no nothin'.

EAMON: You're jokin' me?

OSCAR: Y'timed it brilliantly, it starts first thing in the mornin'.

EAMON: No washin'? I can't do that.

OSCAR: No more sloppin' out either.

EAMON: Ack, Oscar, y'can't be serious. *(Beat.)* What do we do when our piss pots are full?

OSCAR: I don't know but the order is, 'No more sloppin' out.'

EAMON: How long for?

OSCAR: Til we get Political Status back.

EAMON: Jesus.

OSCAR: The plan is to make conditions on the wing so unhygienic, that plagues and infections will run rampant then there will be a massive public outcry, and things will come to a head.

EAMON: That's a truly...truly...mad idea.

OSCAR: Wanna a smoke?

EAMON: Aye!

As he speaks the next section, OSCAR gets off his mattress, squats and begins tugging out a 'parcel' from inside his anus. After a few attempts he is successful. He gets back to the mattress and begins making a few roll-up cigarettes.

OSCAR: Well, we've tried everything else for two years, let's see what happens when the bubonic plague breaks out and half their screws end up in the hospital.

EAMON: But we'll end up in hospital too.

OSCAR: Good. At least we'll have a proper bed. *(Beat.)* There you go, good to hear you joined the IRA at last. None of that oul Auxiliary bollicks.

EAMON is horrified at having to take the cigarette that has just emerged from where it emerged. He slowly cleans the roll-up on his blanket, wiping his hands, etc. OSCAR leans forward with a lit match.

OSCAR: Splunk? *(Gaelic for 'light'.)*

EAMON: Life is full of surprises.

OSCAR: Here, what about m'oul friend Toot McGinley, do y'ever see him?

EAMON: Yeah, used to see Toot all the time.

OSCAR: He was a right clampit, wasn't he?

EAMON: Is Dominic Donnelly still in?

OSCAR: That moonbeam? He got released a lot a months ago. Last I heard he was doin' a degree in medicine at Queen's.

EAMON: What?

OSCAR: Got ye! *(OSCAR laughs.)*

EAMON: What about you? Is your undertaker Da still not speakin' to you?

OSCAR: Thankfully, no.

EAMON: Hey, did you ever see your son again? Damian, was it?

OSCAR: Yeah, Damian.

EAMON: Ever see him again?

OSCAR doesn't answer. He pulls his blanket up around his shoulders and stamps his cigarette butt out on the floor.

FREDDIE: Meanwhile, some other familiar faces were making an appearance in another part of the H Blocks.

FREDDIE leads a hand-cuffed THUMPER into a Waiting Area.

FREDDIE: Back in again then, Thumper?

THUMPER: Ack, just takin' a wee break from the trials and tribulations of shootin' IRA men.

FREDDIE: Eighteen years is a long sentence.

THUMPER: So fuck, if there's two IRA taxi drivers less to worry about.

FREDDIE: The Police were able to connect Thumper to no less than five sectarian murders – but they only had enough evidence to convict him with two.

On a corridor, HANK McNeely stops FREDDIE.

HANK: Oh, Freddie, any word on my guitar?

FREDDIE: None yet, I'm afraid.

HANK: I'm in charge of this wing now Freddie, so I don't want you messin' me about.

FREDDIE: You leave me alone and I'll leave you alone.

HANK: Here, I'm gettin' some books sent up soon. Will you keep an eye out for them?

FREDDIE: What kinda books?

HANK: I'm doin' O levels so m'brother has sent me in some books on sociology. And there's a book on Bob Dylan.

FREDDIE: Your not still a Bob Dylan Fan?

HANK: Tell me a better poet than Dylan? Have you heard a song called 'You're gonna Make Me Lonesome When you Go'?

FREDDIE: Naaa.

HANK: I met this girl Theresa, when I was out, see –
Christmas Eve it was, Lavery's Bar – she leaned in close to my ear and started singin' that song to me – 'You're Gonna Make Me Lonesome When You Go' – the whole song – it was like a dream. I can still smell her perfume – she leaned over into my ear and sang...

HANK starts singing the song, softly at first, then earnestly animating the emotion of the words.

HANK: The only thing about Theresa – she's a member of The Communist Party. *(Beat.)* You'll keep an eye out for the guitar and the books?

FREDDIE: You're wired up, Hank son, wired up.

FREDDIE: It was a surprise when I saw Hank McNeely walkin' back into this prison. I thought he would go on to sort himself out. Instead, he's a top man, now.

HANK meets THUMPER.

THUMPER: Hank! Hank McNeely!

HANK turns round.

HANK: Fuck me! Thumper McKibben. What about ye?

THUMPER: Great.

THUMPER bursts into song, singing 'You Really Got Me'. HANK joins in, before both men burst out laughing and embrace each other warmly.

THUMPER: Good to see you, Hank oul mate.

HANK: You too.

THUMPER: I heard about you getting' arrested. I says d'myself. 'Jesis, it couldn't be Hank McNeely, he's in San Francisco, tunin' in, turnin' on and droppin' out.'

THUMPER roars laughing.

HANK: Well, Thumper, how do you see things goin'?

THUMPER: Awful. It's gonna be a long time before I get m'jamroll again, that's for sure.

HANK: I mean, politically.

THUMPER: Same as ever. The Provos keep bombin' our city and shootin' our peelers, we keep bombin' and shootin' fenians. Is that a difficult one for anybody to understand?

FREDDIE: By the end of 1978 things were really hottin' up in the new H blocks. Republicans had escalated their dirty protest.

STEAL THE SHEETS: They refusing to slop out!

OSCAR: Take that y'bastards!

FREDDIE: Officer Spencer, they're throwin' the piss under the doors!

SPENCER: Brush it back under their doors. Dirty Bastards.

STEAL THE SHEETS and FREDDIE frantically brush the prisoners piss back under their doors.

FREDDIE: Then there was the problem of the number 2 content of their pots. They couldn't get it under the doors so some bright spark had a wonderful idea.

OSCAR: Listen, I'm a republican. Will be til the day I die. But there's no way I'm gonna plaster my own shite on that wall. Tell the OC he can forget that order. No fuckin' way! There's a limit.

FREDDIE: Three days later...

OSCAR is taking great pride in artistically smearing his shit on a wall as he happily hums 'Tears Of A Clown'. At one point some shit falls off his sponge and he steps down off the bed and scrapes it up with his hand and slops it back on the sponge.

OSCAR: Hey, y'wanna see this pattern. It's like a...like a Van Gogh sky. *(Beat.)* This dirty protest isn't so bad after all.

FREDDIE: A few weeks later I was sent into Oscar's cell.

OSCAR: Well, I said to myself, 'If I'm gonna spend the next 10 years of my life in this wee cell I may as well turn it into a home.'

FREDDIE: So he set about decoratin' his cell. Yes, with his own excrement.

OSCAR: The first thing I built was this here mantlepiece. Took me over three days. Then I made this vase of flowers. I thought it looked nice so I put some Chinese ming dynasty patterns on it. Took me over a week.

FREDDIE: Then, to remind him of better times, he made a bottle of Guinness.

OSCAR: Had to put Arthur Guinness' wee signature on it

FREDDIE: In shite. I kid you not.

OSCAR: Then above the fireplace I finished it all off with the three wee geese.

FREDDIE: There they were. The same three geese that flew across everybody's livin' room when we were kids. All made of his own shite. Amazin'.

OSCAR: Could I get an Arts Council grant for this.

FREDDIE: Then the orders came thick and fast. Cut their hair, shave off their beards, forcibly wash them,...

STEAL THE SHEETS places a mirror on the ground.

STEAL THE SHEETS: And we have to put them over this mirror so that we can stop the smugglin'.

SPENCER: Right. Get the bastards out here.

The three Prison Officers approach EAMON and OSCAR's cell. Overseen by SPENCER, FREDDIE and STS enter and drag an unwilling EAMON out. They take him to the washroom where they forcibly wash him with a scrubbing brush. When this is done they drag him across to the other side of the washroom where he is forced to squat over the mirror.

At the end of this, they run him back to his cell but just as they approach the cell, EAMON resists. He pushes FREDDIE hard. This is the cue for FREDDIE and STS to mercilessly beat EAMON into his cell. OSCAR intervenes and gets the same treatment. The Prison Officers leave. EAMON and OSCAR lie motionless on the floor. After a moment, EAMON lifts his head. He yells at the prison door.

EAMON: Heyyyyyyyy! Yiz are scum! Evil fuckers! Psychopaths. You can't be a screw and be a good person. It's a fuckin' contradiction. We are striving for freedom and human liberty – and yous bastards revel in being cruel to defenceless men. Scum. Scum. Bastard scum!!!

FREDDIE: *(Breathless.)* That night, a lot of prisoners resisted and they were beat like never before. Normally, after a confrontation, the republicans would be up to their cell doors and before y'knew it, they'd be singin and banterin' of some sort.

EAMON: Oscar? Oscar? Get up to your door and get the lads lifted.

OSCAR: Leave it, Eamon. I'm fucked.

EAMON crawls over to the pipes and shouts.

EAMON: Davy Dolan, give is a song, big lad?

Silence.

FREDDIE: This night, not one of them moved from their mattresses. There was an eerie silence on the block. Then, about half an hour later.

DAVY: *(Shouting from another cell.)* Oscar! Oscar, mo chara?

OSCAR: Hello Davy?

DAVY: Just got word from H6.

OSCAR: What?

DAVY: The Hunger-strike's on.

EAMON: Holy Jesus. A Hunger Strike?

Unsteadily, OSCAR gets up. He drags and cajoles EAMON to his feet. He grips him at the back of the neck and looks into his face.

OSCAR: Are y'with me, Eamon.

EAMON looks back at OSCAR and grips him in return.

EAMON: I'm with you, our kid.

OSCAR: Ok. Lets get these lads lifted

OSCAR goes over to his cell door. With his hands he begins beatin' out a hard, but steady, rhythm on the cell door. He begins singing Free's 'Alright Now'. As he sings the others enourage and urge him on.

ARTIE: *(From another cell.)* Ya, billy oscar!

ARTIE and DAVY cheer. The other prisoners begin to stir and we hear shouts from other cells.

ARTIE: Chuckie ar la!

ARTIE joins in the singing.

DAVY: C'mon Oscar, let it rip!

DAVY & WOODEN SPOON, another prisoner in another cell, cheer.

OSCAR turns to face EAMON and they sing the next line into each other's faces.

Soon, dozens of prisoners are up at their cell doors joinin' in on the chorus and bangin' to the rhythm. It becomes like a rallying call, reaching an emotional climax, with the prisoners singing at the top of their voices, almost frightenin' in its intensity.

BLACKOUT

ACT 2

The republican prisoners are in their cells.

OSCAR: Okay, everybody! It's eight a clock. The bears are off the wing. Oscar's up at the window...and it's party time!!!

DOMINIC: Go asleep, Oscar!

OSCAR: It's your DJ with charees-may, your MC with personal-a-tee! And the show that brings you the very best in entertainment! Radio Long Kesh!

EAMON: Oscar, there's an Irish class startin' shortly!

OSCAR: Fuck the Irish class! I wanna bit a craic! Here, Wooden Spoon! Wooden, come up to the cell door a minute! Tell is about the time y'robbed the Post Office in Newry and yiz came away with 400 Family Allowance books and twenty seven second class stamps!

WOODEN SPOON: Who? All your good for Oscar, is pullin' your plonker!

OSCAR: It's better than bein' a plonker!

EAMON: Oscar, we had Bobby telling us the story of Spartacus last week, Tommy McKearney wants to tell us the story of The Boer War.

OSCAR: Fuck off. He spent two weeks telling us that over in H6 and believe you me, it was a bore.

OSCAR: *(Radio disc jockey voice.)* You're listenin' to Radio Long Kesh with me Oscar, the Dee Jay with chareesmay, the MC with personal-a-tee, and the show that brings you all the very best in entertainment! For the next hour and a half you'll be entertained by some of the shitiest, smelliest, ugliest bastards ever to don a felon's blanket. All to get one thing – Political Status. Right, now...

WOODEN SPOON: Oscar, give us some Tamla Motown!

OSCAR: No, we're gonna have Artie McCracken from the Glens Of Antrim to sing Roisin d'focka weel ya!

Loud cheering and applause.

OSCAR: C'mon Artie, you're on the air!

ARTIE: This is for all Glens of Antrim people, at home and abroad.

WOODEN SPOON: Pile of culchies!

ARTIE: *(Threateningly.)* I'll see you later, Wooden Spoon.

(Big cheer from others.)

'Óró 's é do bheatha 'bhaile...
Óró 's é do bheatha 'bhaile
Óró 's é do bheatha 'bhaile
Anois ar theacht an tsamhraidh...'

ARTIE: *(Shouting.)* Up the Provos and up the 'dall!

There is cheering and applauding. Suddenly, noises are heard.

OSCAR: Hold it lads! Shuuush!

EAMON: Somebody out there.

OSCAR: Somebody squeaky bootin'?

EAMON: Bears in the air! Bears in the air!

We hear loud footsteps, the jangling of keys and gates opening and banging. The men listen intently at their doors. TOOT McGinley is escorted onto the wing by FREDDIE.

TOOT: Is there any way I could keep m'jeans and wear them under m'blanket?

FREDDIE: That's up to your OC, not me.

OSCAR: I know that voice.

EAMON: That's Toot McGinley!

OSCAR: Holy Jesis!

EAMON: What about ye, Toot son?

TOOT: Is that you, Eamon Jennings?

FREDDIE: Keep it quiet, McGinley!

EAMON: You joinin' the blanket men, Toot?

TOOT: Whadaya want me to do? I might be innocent but I'm still a republican, amn't a?

Great cheers and applause from the men.

Up the Provos! Up the Blanket men!!

OSCAR: Toot M'fuckin' Ginley.

FREDDIE places TOOT in a cell and walks towards exit.

You okay Toot?

FREDDIE: Alright, keep it down in there!

FREDDIE exits.

TOOT: Oscar Coyle, that you y'Derry dirtbird?

OSCAR: Yes Toot, definitely me.

EAMON: What were y'done for, Toot son?

TOOT: Bombin' the Europa Hotel. But Eamon, I'm completely innocent!

OSCAR: Again!

TOOT: A bomb went off down town and blew up the Europa Hotel and the Grand Opera House. The said the found my fingerprints and hair samples in the getaway car.

EAMON: Toot, it's hard to dispute fingerprints and hair.

TOOT: I'm not disputin' them. The car was m'uncle Charlie's.

EAMON: And you'd been in it?

TOOT: Loads a times.

OSCAR: Here Toot, we're havin' a sing song. Will y'give us a song?

TOOT: Me? I can't sing.

OSCAR: Y'used to sing in the cages.

TOOT: I'm a crap singer.

OSCAR: I know that, but that's not the issue. In here everybody gets to do their party piece. Everybody gets heard. Let's have a song, Toot oul son.

TOOT: Ok. This is for my wife, Rosie.

OSCAR: The fucker's married! Toot McGinley's got a woman!

TOOT begins to sing 'Sugar Sugar' – very badly, tuneless. He mimics instrumental sections with his mouth. He dances a nice tidy neat little mod dance.

Toot's singing is immediately met with the most cruel derision, i.e. jeering, raspberries, shouting, banging, etc.

TOOT stops singing in the face of the derision.

TOOT: Yiz bastards!

Laughter all round. Lights down. Passage of time. It is late at night. The cast sing softly, gently.

EAMON: Toot! Toot you awake?

TOOT: Yis. That you, Eamon?

EAMON: Yis. Down to the pipes.

The two men lie flat on the floor down beside the heating pipes connecting their prison wall.

You alright?

TOOT: Can't sleep.

EAMON: Y'say you were framed for the Europa?

TOOT: Honest d'god, Eamon. You know I would tell you if I was involved. I'd just got married. We were plannin' d'move to Blackburn where her Aunt Kathleen lives. I am completely innocent. Now, I'm starin' at eight bowlers.

EAMON: Well, at least you'll have Rosie to come and visit ye and everything.

TOOT: Not only that, she's expectin'.

EAMON: You're jokin' me.

TOOT: Everything okay between you and Cathy?

EAMON: Well, I haven't seen her in nearly 18 months if that's any indication.

TOOT: Yous fell out?

EAMON: That's one way of puttin' it. She refuses to visit while I'm on the Blanket.

TOOT: Y'know I used d'see Cathy nearly every day when she was leavin' the kids up to school?

EAMON: Yeah, I heard that.

TOOT: Y'know I was workin' as the school caretaker, don't ya?

EAMON: Course a do.

TOOT: Your kids are great, Eamon. Energy d'burn, the have. The wee one, Conan. He was always comin' up d'me, know on his way into school with Cathy, and he'd say, 'Toot, I bet ye you don't know how to make a ten pee disappear'. And he would do a wee trick for me and make his ten pee disappear. Cathy's great too. Maybe she'll come up to visit you soon.

EAMON: I wouldn't hold m'breath.

TOOT: You haven't seen the kids in 18 months either?

EAMON: No. She won't let the kids see me like this.

TOOT: That's terrible. *(Beat.)* Here Eamon. How did you get to be OC of the wing? I remember you tellin' me you were never gonna join the army.

EAMON: A lot has happened, Toot. Ten years ago, my priorities were to buy a house and provide a good life for my wife and family. Then the Troubles erupted. Now my number one priority is to fight Margaret Thatcher and win political status for these men. Things happen. It's the old John Lennon thing. Life is what happens while you're makin' plans for the future.

TOOT: And you're OC of a whole Wing, nigh.

EAMON: Yeah, I'm in charge of forty eight men. Most of them are lookin' at bein' here for the best part of their adult lives, and some of them are about to embark on a hunger strike.

TOOT: Hunger strike? What are you on about, hunger-strike?

EAMON: Try and get some sleep, Toot son. Sleep is a prisoner's best friend. See y'in the mornin'.

TOOT: Night, Eamon. *(Beat.)* Oh, Eamon?

EAMON: Yes?

TOOT: Is there any seagulls about the H Blocks?

EAMON: It's not seagulls I'm thinkin' about, Toot son. Good night.

EAMON gently sings The Beatles' 'All My Loving'. During this, we see the prisoners restless, as they try to sleep.

FREDDIE: Alec Spencer gave the Prison Service a bad name. He spent even more time in the Prison Social Club than me.

STEAL THE SHEETS and FREDDIE are talking as they share guard duty.

STEAL THE SHEETS: Did a tell ye I've put in for a job in the Post Office?

FREDDIE: The Post Office?

STS: Fed up with this. Up to our oxters in Falls Road shite every day of the week

SPENCER enters. He looks through the flap into the cell of EAMON and OSCAR.

SPENCER: C'mon yous two. I need yiz for a wee job.

They follow SPENCER to the cells. SPENCER stops at OSCAR's cell.

SPENCER: Open this door.

STEAL THE SHEETS opens the door. SPENCER enters. He proceeds to beat up OSCAR. He stops and leaves OSCAR lying on the ground. He walks on to the next cell and points to the lock.

SPENCER: Way y'go.

STEAL THE SHEETS: Alec, y'can't do this. It's eleven a clock at night.

STEAL THE SHEETS continues to open the cell door. SPENCER is seething with anger.

SPENCER: Open the fuckin' door! Look. These prisoners are bastards.

He enters the cell and physically abuses a prisoner.

These fuckers have walked into peoples living rooms...

He speaks as he perpetrates viciousness on the prisoner.

SPENCER: ...and shot fathers in slow motion in front of their wives and children. Left bombs knowing innocent people were goin' to be killed. They are scum, low life scum.

SPENCER leaves the prisoner lying on the floor and exits the cell.

FREDDIE: Alec come on.

SPENCER bangs a cell door and shouts.

FREDDIE: We managed to get him stopped after he'd beaten five prisoners. Meanwhile, the up and coming Twelth of July celebrations was of more importance to Loyalists than any republican hunger-strike.

FREDDIE enters.

FREDDIE: Visit for McKibben! Visit for McKibben!

THUMPER: That's me.

THUMPER jumps to his feet and starts grooming himself.

HANK: Who's visitin'?

THUMPER: Juicy Lucy. Remember the cop's daughter? From Comber?

HANK: You lucky bastard.

THUMPER: I have requested a 'Welfare' visit with my 'sister' Lucy, meaning I will be able to close the Cubicle door behind me for some 'family' privacy.

HANK: If only I could get Theresa to visit me.

THUMPER: You still in touch with Theresa The Commie?

HANK: I'm afraid she's the love of my life. *(Beat.)* Don't forget, we have a staff meeting at four a'clock this afternoon. To plan the Twelfth celebrations.

THUMPER: Righhhht! I'm in charge of makin' the hooch.

HANK: Never mind makin' the drink, you are in charge of gettin' the Band rehearsed.

THUMPER: This is – the two hundred and ninetieth anniversary of the Battle Of The Boyne – we'll need to make loads of drink.

HANK: Right Lads!

HANK jumps to his feet and the Band assembles.

BAND MEMBER: What is it, The Sash?

HANK: Yes, The Sash. Form up, lads!

The Band plays The Sash. HANK steps forward and expertly performs a skilled routine with the Band mace stick, throwing it above his head, etc.

FREDDIE: The Twelfth of July duly came round. A ridiculous amount of alcohol was both home-brewed and smuggled in. So much, that the Governor decided enough was enough.

Prison officers hurry into loyalist wing.

THUMPER: The screws are raidin'! Everybody up to the gate, lads!

HANK: Keep them out! Fenian bastards!

There is hand to hand fighting/struggling as the Prison Officers are forced out. The Loyalist prisoners begin to barricade themselves in their wing.

THUMPER: Get the snooker tables, table tennis tables, block the gate!

HANK: They're tryin' to stop us celebratin' our heritage! C'mon!

THUMPER: No surrender!

More loud loyalist band music. Prison Officer SPENCER enters.

ALL: *Hello Hello we are the Billy Boys*
Hello Hello you'll know us by our noise
Cause we're up to our necks in Fenian blood
Surrender or you'll die
We are the Shankill Billy Boys

FREDDIE: After several hours the Governor himself appeared.

A prisoner sings a line from 'Hey Hey We're The Monkees'.

GOVERNOR: Prisoner McNeely?

HANK is drunk out of his mind. He has to work hard to steady himself and stay standing up straight. His speech is slurred.

HANK: That's me.

GOVERNOR: You in charge of these prisoners?

HANK: That's right, Commanding Office...office...office...cer.

GOVERNOR: You're drunk.

HANK: If you were me, you'd be drunk too.

GOVERNOR: I must tell you I want this disturbance brought to an end immediately and this wing returned to normal.

HANK: If there's no parade, there'll be...no normal.

FREDDIE: Negotiations broke down, but an hour later the Governor was back.

GOVERNOR: I'm prepared to let you have a short parade providing no music is played and all alcohol is removed from the wing.

HANK: No music or drink on the Twelfth? Sure that would be like tryin' to sing Bob Dylan songs without the words.

HANK starts singing Bob Dylan's 'A Hard Rain's a-Gonna Fall' angrily into the GOVERNOR's face.

Throughout the singing the GOVERNOR barks out orders to his staff.

GOVERNOR: PO Carson! Call in the Riot Squad! Officer Gillespie! Inform the Northern Ireland Office we are going in!

HANK continues to sing.

FREDDIE: A compromise was eventually reached and by tea-time that day the disturbance was over. Over in the Republican blocks the dirty protest was reachin' its climax.

EAMON, OSCAR and TOOT are up at their cell doors. The mood is very solemn.

EAMON: Everybody understand everything I've just said?

OSCAR: Yeah, no problem Eamon.

EAMON: Toot?

TOOT: Yis.

EAMON: The OC wants the names of the men volunteering to go on the Hunger Strike finalised for this Friday. You're only to put your name forward if you are absolutely sure you're prepared to go the whole way. They don't want no fuckin' about here.

Silence.

TOOT: I won't be puttin' my name down, lads. Eamon, I'm a cowardly bastard.

EAMON: Toot, nobody expected you to put your name forward. You're not even in the Ra.

TOOT: Besides Eamon, I got some bad news last night.

EAMON: What's that?

TOOT: Rosie lost our baby.

EAMON: Ah Jesis, Toot son. Sorry to hear about that. But here, you've no need to get involved in any of this, Toot. *(Beat.)* What about you, Oscar?

OSCAR: Can I get back to you, Eamon?

EAMON: No problem, no problem. As I said. We've up to Friday.

TOOT: Eamon, you can't do it either. You have a wife and two kids.

EAMON: I'll take my decision by Friday too. Okay, lads?

FREDDIE: The situation in the prison was becoming unbearable. I'd already had a couple of threats on my own life and I would waken up in the mornin's and go, 'Ah shit! I have d'go d'work.' *(Beat.)* Come Friday, the republican were deciding who was to live and who was to die.

EAMON is dozing on his mattress. OSCAR has been awake, thinking.

OSCAR: Eamon?

EAMON: Yes, Oscar.

OSCAR: I've taken my decision. *(Beat.)* I'm gonna leave it.

EAMON: No problem, mo chara.

OSCAR: Y'know I don't agree with it in the first place – as a tactic like. And I wouldn't be up to it.

EAMON: Fully understood, Oscar.

OSCAR: But send me on a special mission to get into Margaret Thatcher's bedroom and kill her with my own bare hands and I'm your man, know what a mean?

EAMON: Horses for courses, Oscar, what?

OSCAR: What about you?

EAMON: I've decided to put my name in the hat.

OSCAR: Fucksake, Eamon. Why?

EAMON: It has to be done.

OSCAR: This is your life you're talkin' about here.

EAMON: We can't let Margaret Thatcher win.

OSCAR: Fuck Margaret Thatcher. There's other ways of beatin' this.

EAMON: We've tried everything over four years.

OSCAR: You know I've always advocated goin' into the Prison system and wreckin' it from inside.

EAMON: Nobody has any faith in that.

OSCAR: Look, there's five or six hundred republican prisoners. If we refuse to work the system, there can't be any system. We have to use our fuckin' brains for once. Play the bastards at their own game. Eamon nobody has to die.

EAMON: Oscar, Oscar, Oscar you're missin' the point. This is the British imperial establishment. They are tryin' to win the war through the prisons. This is not just about food and prison uniforms and how many letters we can receive. This is about the War. The 800 year-old war between England and Ireland. If we are defeated inside, it will have huge implications for the prosecution of the War outside.

OSCAR: I'm only sayin', we fight it a different way. A more cunning way. We shouldn't be so fuckin' brave for a start.

EAMON: Besides, I couldn't let a bunch of screw bastards treat me like I'm a purse thief.

OSCAR: I know all that, but...

EAMON: And anyway. The aim is to get enough support on the outside so that Thatcher will give in before anyone has to die.

OSCAR: Eamon, please don't put your name forward?

EAMON: It's done.

OSCAR: You're a bastard. I'm beggin' you. This is shit.

EAMON: I told you, it'll work out fine.

OSCAR: Y'know, I've spent nearly all my years in jail with you.

EAMON: Coyle, you're not getting' all sentimental on me? Of all people!

OSCAR: Eamon, please take your fuckin' name off the list.

EAMON: I'm gonna have a kip now.

OSCAR: Okay, okay, here's the deal. I'm gonna kill you. I'm gonna find a way of killing you so that you won't be able to die on hunger-strike.

EAMON laughs loudly.

FREDDIE: Eamon Jennings went to bed that night determined to put his name down for the hunger strike. But next mornin'?

EAMON: Oscar?

OSCAR: Hello, sir.

EAMON: Just lettin' you know I never slept a wink last night.

OSCAR: What?

EAMON: I'm not puttin' my name forward. *(Beat.)* Oscar?

OSCAR: You are one big, hairy, gabshite bastard of a plonker! You've had me up half the fuckin' night plannin' your funeral. I was carrying your coffin up the falls road! I'm gonna break every bone in your body!

FREDDIE: Even though we all knew the hunger strike was comin', it still didn't prepare us for when it actually happened. Alec Spencer was in his element.

Prison Officer SPENCER carries a plate of food into a hunger-striker's cell. He holds the plate out to the prisoner.

SPENCER: There y'go boy. A lovely plate of roast chicken, with roast potatoes, carrots, parsnip and lovely onion gravy.

The Prisoner doesn't move other than to shake his head.

SPENCER: Ach What? Don't want it?

SPENCER leans down to the food and sniffs deeply.

Alright. I'll leave it over here. Don't worry, we won't say a word if there's a wee leg of chicken missing when we come back. *(Under his breath.)* Cunt.

SPENCER leaves the cell.

FREDDIE: By the time the hunger strike entered its fourth week, the tension in the whole community was reaching an all-time high.

NEWSREADER: Here is the news.

Following a rally in West Belfast in support of the seven hunger strikers at The Maze Prison, there has been widespread rioting in many parts of Northern Ireland. One person has been killed and several Police Officers injured when...

FREDDIE: Outside, on the issue of the Hunger strike, the community was split perfectly down the middle.

Two men appear on opposite sides of the stage and begin painting slogans on the wall.

NATIONALIST PAINTER: Support...the...seven...brave... hunger...strikers.

LOYALIST PAINTER: Let...the...murderin'...bastards...die.

FREDDIE: After 42 days, rumours were sweepin' the prison that hunger striker Sean McKenna was close to death.

An anxious doctor hurries into the room. He approaches EAMON. There is a flurry of Paramedic and prisoner activity nearby.

PRISONER 1: What did you hear?

PRISONER 2: Sean McKenna has lost his eye sight.

PRISONER 1: You're joking me!

DOCTOR: Mister Jennings, I have to advise you that Sean McKenna's condition has deteriorated sharply.

ORDERLY 1: Ambulance is waiting outside!

DOCTOR: We're taking him to intensive care.

ORDERLY 2: Message to the front gate. Prisoner McKenna on his way!

ORDERLY 3: Heart beat still fluctuating

FREDDIE: Family have arrived

DOCTOR: I would like permission to save this man's life.

Sean McKenna is wheeled past them by orderlies. The doctor looks at EAMON pleadingly. The trolley stops. All eyes are on EAMON. EAMON stares resolutely ahead, before speaking.

EAMON: The Dark says, 'feed him'.

DOCTOR: Thank you. *(Shouting to others.)* Prepare for intravene! Blood pressure, please?

ORDERLY 2: Page Doctor Fitzpatrick

ORDERLY 3: On that right away

Another flurry of activity as Sean McKenna is rushed to intensive care.

FREDDIE: In the meantime, the Brits had promised the Prisoners a document that appeared to settle things. On the strength of this, the Prisoners called off the Hunger-strike.

THUMPER: So. They're feedin' Sean McKenna as we speak. I had a hundred fegs on the bastard snuffin' it by 12 a clock the marra. Shitbags.

HANK is silent.

What's wrong you?

HANK: Got a letter from Theresa.

THUMPER: Theresa The Commie? The love of your life who never comes to visit you?

HANK: It's a Dear John.

HANK buries his head in his hands.

FREDDIE: At the chapel that Sunday the republicans gathered as usual to hear the crack. For a moment we thought we could return to normal.

OSCAR: What did Bobby say?

EAMON: Another hunger-strike.

TOOT: Serious?

EAMON: Only this time, he says, we have to see it through.

FREDDIE: So. The Brits wanted total control of the prison and the Provos insisted on every single one of their demands. Result: Stalemate.

OSCAR and EAMON are up at their cell doors.

EAMON: Second hunger-strike starts Monday week. This time we're not puttin' seven men on at the same time. We're goin' to stagger it – one startin' every fortnight – so as to ensure it lasts and we put maximum pressure on Maggie Thatcher.

OSCAR: Bobby goin' first?

EAMON: Bobby goin' first.

OSCAR: What about you?

EAMON: I've put my name down.

OSCAR: For fucksake, Eamon.

EAMON: Don't worry, I'm number fourteen or something. Not much Bob Hope of it reachin' me.

OSCAR: Does Cathy know you've put your name down?

EAMON: She will know by the time she comes up to visit.

FREDDIE: Unbelievably, the second hunger-strike was creating even more tension than the first. For a period, the hospital wing seemed like Piccadilly Circus.

A parade of would-be peacemakers approach EAMON.

DUBLIN: You can rest assured the Irish Government is doin' all in its power to persuade the British Government to end this hunger strike.

EAMON: Thanks.

BISHOP: Just to let you know son, that as we speak, the Vatican is exchanging documents with Downing St. and we're all praying for a solution.

EAMON: Appreciate that, Father.

SDLP: You boys don't seem to want to compromise. If you would drop even one of your demands? We in the SDLP…

EAMON: No.

PRIEST: Taking your own life is a sin in the eyes of the Catholic Church.

EAMON: Up yours too.

EUROPEAN: The European Parliament have been given a guarantee from the British Government that if you drop the work demand, they'll give you the rest.

EAMON: Could we have that in writin'?

IRA MAN: The Leadership on the outside says, 'hold your ground'. Ok?

EAMON: I'm your man.

We hear the soft playing of 'Annie's Song' on the flute. Lights fade up. It is HANK.

THUMPER: What are y'doin' playin' that shite?

HANK: If it's good enough for James Galway it's good enough for me.

THUMPER: He's another one. Learned everything he knew in an orange band but y'wouldn't hear him playin' The Sash on The Val Doonican Show, would ye? No, siree.

HANK: I wonder what's the latest on Sands?

THUMPER: Who cares?

HANK: Thumper, still no chance of you puttin' your name down for the Open University thing?

THUMPER: You away in the head? University's only for people who don't know things.

HANK: It's you who's losin' out. There's five in the cage startin' next week.

THUMPER: Good luck to yiz.

HANK: The CO says he wants us to find out why we're fighin' for loyalism. He says the loyalist working class have to start relyin' on themselves, instead of always voting for solicitors and businessmen in the Unionist Party.

THUMPER: The CO's head's full of wee white mice.

HANK: Even Theresa says there'd be no point in us havin' a relationship if I don't get educated. Tell me this Thumper? How do you know you're in love?

THUMPER: How the fuck would I know?

HANK: You don't love Lucy?

THUMPER: Juicy Lucy the cop's daughter, are you off your head? Did I not tell you she sent a letter up last week sayin' she had a baby two months ago – and it's mine.

FREDDIE: The arguments continued to rage, but in spite of all the last minute efforts to end the hunger strike, the news seeped through in the early hours of the mornin'.

EAMON gets up to his door.

EAMON: Toot! Up to the door.

TOOT: Yes, Eamon.

EAMON: It's all over. Bobby passed away a few minutes ago.

TOOT: Ah Jesis.

In a loud, powerful and emotional voice OSCAR begins singing Sam Cooke's 'A Change Is Gonna Come'.

The singing is interspersed by interruptions from the prisoners.

TOOT: Hail Mary, full of grace, the Lord is with thee
blessed art thou among women
and blessed is the fruit of thy womb, Jesus...

SPENCER: Steal The Sheets! Did you hear the terrible news?

STS: Is it true then, Alex?

SPENCER: It better be, because they're makin' arrangements
to bury him!

SPENCER and STS laugh heartily.

TOOT: Eamon? Are y'watchin' the seagulls?

EAMON: I am.

TOOT: They know, don't the?

EAMON: They do, Toot. They know, ok.

FREDDIE: At this stage, the pressure in that place was so bad
I lifted a bible I found in the locker room and started
reading it every chance a got. Nothin' serious, just
something to take m'mind off things. Nobody had any idea
Bobby Sands would only be the first of ten. Ten?

EAMON is making a speech in commemoration of Francis Hughes. At other points in the prison, via various sources, the deaths of the other hunger-strikers are announced.

EAMON: We are gathered here today to honour the memory
of Francis Hughes, a great republican and an exceptional
volunteer...

THUMPER: *(Singing.)*
> *'Yippedy yep sir, that's my wish, do dah, do dah*
> *Number three, fuckface McCreesh, doh da, doh da day...'*

NEWSREADER: Londonderry INLA man, Patsy O'Hara became the fourth hunger-striker to die...

OSCAR sings the first line from 'The Ballad of Joe McDonnell'.

TOOT: Martin Hurson? Poor Barabus? I shared a cell with him. *(Laughing.)* Worse two weeks of my life.

TORY POLITICIAN: I see here in the *Times*, a seventh hunger-striker, Kevin Lynch has just killed himself. One thing these people don't know about Margaret, she won't be bettered.

OSCAR: Two facts I'll never forget. Big Doc and the second of August, 1981. May you rest in peace, comrade mor.

THUMPER: *(Singing.)*
> *'Yippedy yep, he's had his tea, do dah, do dah*
> *Number nine, big McIlwee, do dah, do dah day...'*

NEWSREADER: Following the death of a tenth hunger-striker, Michael Devine...

The various sources start repeating snatches of their announcements, overlapping with each other, until it reaches a crescendo. FREDDIE enters downstage. He is very drunk.

FREDDIE: It's over then!

The crescendo comes to an abrupt halt. Silence.

All over and done. Ten men tatty bread and down the big bury hole. Ten men. Know what I say? Damn everybody. Everybody. Maggie Thatcher, the Irish Government, the IRA, the Governor of the Maze. And some Prison Officers got away with behavin' like animals. Fuck – can I say that word? – fuck the hunger-strikers. Fuck everybody who had anything to do with it, for causin' so much pain to so many people, especially to the families of the hunger-strikers.

No cause is worth what those people went through. Damn the whole thing for causin' all the people on the outside to be killed as well. Everybody forgets about them, the ordinary Joe Soaps. They died too. *(Beat.)* That's what I say. But this is only my opinion. Who cares what I think? I'm only Freddie Gillespie, a wee 'nobody screw'. That's me. Freddie the 'nobody', who means nothin' to nobody. But I know things. I was there too. *(Beat.)* Did y'hear about the wife? Maureen? Left me again. Last week. Took Alan and Ruth with her this time. Says this time it's for good. *(Dramatically takes out his hand gun.)* This is all I have left. A Walther PPK automatic pistol. For my personal protection. My personal 'protection'? I was cleanin' it last night – I had drink on me, of course – I was cleanin' it last night and I looked at it sittin' in the palm of my hand and I thought to myself, I thought to myself – *(He brings the gun up, pointing under his chin.)* 'do I have to live like this forever'? *(His head snaps back, like it was a failed attempt to shoot himself.)* But – it's for 'my personal protection'. *(Again, his head snaps back.)* Y'see, when you own a gun, it doesn't just sit in your pocket, or in the wardrobe or wherever you keep it. It sits here. *(Becoming emotional, he taps the centre of his forehead repeatedly.)* It's too powerful to just sit where you put it. It moves to here by itself. *(Taps his forehead again.)* But there y'go. It's all over. There's ten men dead inside and 67 dead outside and I'm a ragin' drunk. Not even good enough to hold on to my wife and kids.

EAMON and TOOT are making tea. DOMINIC is standing at the cell door talking to them.

TOOT: Imagine? A man at your age, Dominic, startin' into a third prison sentence.

DOMINIC: But that judge knew I hadn't been active since the seventies. He knew about my migraines, knew I had terrible bad gout – and knew about the arthritis in the hip. And he still gave me eight years!

TOOT: Yes, but y'had four armalites in your house.

DOMINIC: Yes, but the weren't mine!

EAMON: Don't worry Dominic, four years'll fly by. Wanna cup of tea?

DOMINIC: Naa, fuck tea.

DOMINIC exits.

FREDDIE: So, the republican prisoners were, at last, settlin' down.
They had got most of the original five demands but it wasn't shouted from the rooftops. Sorry, did you just hear me say the republican prisoners were settlin' down?

TOOT: Okay, I've to watch everything, what time the food lorry arrives and departs, don't write anything down, just register it up here, *(Taps his temple.)* watch how Steal The Sheets communicates with the driver. Is it the same driver every day or different drivers? Right?

EAMON: Spot on. And remember. Spread the word around there's to be no confrontations with the screws. Right? Just 'how y'doin' Officer so-and-so, yes sir, no sir, three bags full, sir.' Okay?

TOOT: Okay. *(Beat.)* Did I tell ye, I've started a letters campaign to Belfast City Council to have the term 'Bealfierstian' officially recognised?

EAMON: Outta here.

TOOT: I'm goin'. *(Beat.)* Oh, I told Oscar you wanted him to come up and see you, but he says to tell you, he'll be in his cell if you want him.

EAMON: Did he?

TOOT exits. EAMON approaches Oscar's cell with a cup of tea for OSCAR, singing 'The Town I Loved So Well' as he enters. OSCAR is lying on his bed.

EAMON enters the cell. He nudges the sleeping OSCAR.

Here, Phil Coulter, a cup of char for ya.

He sets a cup of tea down beside OSCAR. OSCAR stirs and sits up. He doesn't look at EAMON or show much interest.

OSCAR: Thanks, Eamon.

EAMON: Ok, what goin' on, Oscar mate?

OSCAR: Not a lot.

EAMON: Where is our bestest, sexiest, Entertainment Officer? Our DJ with charees-may? Where has the cheeky chappie we all knew and loved gone? Eh?

OSCAR: Eamon, I'm not in the form for any of this.

EAMON: Any communication from the Maiden city these days?

OSCAR: Me Da wants a visit.

EAMON: That's great news.

OSCAR: Says he wants to get back on terms with me.

EAMON: You'll send him out a visit?

OSCAR: I'll think about it.

EAMON: Good. I think you should. Might help you to get things together, might be…might be the lift you need.

OSCAR: Who said I needed a lift.

EAMON: Oscar, some of the men are tellin' me you're not even lookin' after your basic hygiene.

OSCAR: Fuck the men.

EAMON: *(Angrily.)* No, fuck you.

OSCAR jumps to his feet and confronts EAMON angrily.

OSCAR: Fuck me? Whadaya mean, fuck me?

EAMON: I mean, fuck you! Fuck this *(Looking around the cell.)* Fuck all this hermit stuff.

OSCAR: It's none of your business.

EAMON: It is my Business.

OSCAR: It's not.

EAMON: While I'm OC of this Wing, it is.

OSCAR: I used to be your OC.

EAMON: That's right. That was the old Oscar. The new Oscar isn't fit to be OC of a dog kennel.

Silence. OSCAR flops down on his seat. EAMON gets in close. He speaks softly.

Mo chara? What can I do to help? You name it mate, and if there's anything I can do, let's get it done.

Silence.

OSCAR: Can y'bring Bobby back? *(Beat.)* And Joe? *(Beat.)* And all the rest of the boys? Can y'get Damian back from Wales?

EAMON: No, you know I can't.

OSCAR: Then end of story.

OSCAR drops his head and stares at the floor.

EAMON: No, not end of story. This is the beginnin' of the story. We were all wrecked by the boys dyin'. But we have to go forward. The lads wouldn't have wanted you to go like this.

OSCAR: It wasn't worth it, Eamon. I've lay in bed night after night and I can't get my head round it. Can't...can't accept it.

EAMON: Okay Oscar, here's the deal. Listen to me. *(Beat.)* It doesn't matter if it was worth it. It doesn't matter if we got this and didn't get that. What matters...what really matters is that it's over. That doesn't mean we forget the lads who died. Far from it. But what matters now is the future. Yous. Mine. And all the other men runnin' about out there. And our families. *(Beat.)* And besides. You're the most important man in the jail right now.

OSCAR looks up at EAMON.

I need your help, Oscar.

OSCAR: I'm won't be doin' anything, Eamon. I thought I'd made that clear.

EAMON: We're plannin' something big and we need your help.

OSCAR: Plan it without me.

EAMON: An escape.

OSCAR: Escape?

EAMON: A big one. Anything up to ten, twenty, thirty men – maybe even forty.

OSCAR: You're nuts.

EAMON: Oscar, we're goin' out. It's the best plan I've ever came across. We're that *(Snaps his fingers.)* close to pullin' it off. We just need one or two last wee pieces to fall into place. And that's where you come in.

OSCAR: And what would that be?

EAMON: A concert. We want you to organise a big concert to allow us to distract the screws so that we can get our hands on a couple of things. What do you say?

OSCAR: A concert? Singin' and everything?

EAMON: The heap.

OSCAR: Holy shit.

EAMON: Only we don't want none of that Smokey Robinson, Tamla Motown shit.

OSCAR looks at him aghast.

Only jokin' ya!

Both men laugh.

Are we on?

EAMON holds out his hand. OSCAR looks at it, then shakes it.

OSCAR: Trust a brilliant escape to come up when I'm due to be released. Just my luck.

EAMON: Better scoot.

TOOT: Oscar! Oscar, where the hell are you? The concert was supposed to start ten minutes ago!

OSCAR: I'm comin, I'm comin!

OSCAR rushes onstage. EAMON, TOOT, DOMINIC and some other prisoners are already on the stage vocalising a bass beat for the forthcoming song, 'This Old Heart Of Mine'. FREDDIE is in the front row of the audience really enjoying himself.

OSCAR: Oscar has entered the building! Okay, ladies and gentlemen...

FREDDIE: There's no women here!

OSCAR: Except for you Freddie, y'big girl's blouse!

FREDDIE roars laughing.

Okay everybody settle down, it's Oscar here, your MC with person–al–it–tee. Your DJ with charees-may! Are you ready to party! Our first song is a special request for Freddie Gillespie down at the front here, the only person in the whole of Long Kesh – prisoner or screw – who supports Everton!

Everybody laughs. OSCAR takes lead vocals with backing from EAMON, TOOT, DOMINIC and the others, comprising a well-rehearsed dance routine, with plenty of fun and messing, etc. They sing 'This Old Heart Of Mine'.

As the NEWSREADER is heard, the singers stop singing but lean to one side and continue to click their fingers in unison.

NEWSREADER: Now here is the News. Reports are coming in of a mass escape by prisoners at the Maze Prison. Thirty eight prisoners are unaccounted for and a widespread security operation has been set up around the prison. The Secretary of State has said...

The men resume singing and finish the song. The concert is over.

Later, OSCAR enters carrying his black bag of worldly goods over his shoulder. EAMON arrives to meet him. The two men stare at each other for a moment.

EAMON: Okay, mo chara?

OSCAR: Y'know me. *(Cagney-esque.)* 'On top of the world, Ma.'

EAMON: So you finally got your release papers. In twenty minutes time you'll be speedin' down the M2 motorway.

OSCAR: Yeah. Back to 'Coyle's Funeral Parlour – keen prices and discreet services guaranteed.'

FREDDIE enters.

FREDDIE: Transport for Oliver Coyle! Okay, Oscar?

FREDDIE moves off. TOOT enters.

TOOT: Okay, Oscar.

TOOT walks straight up to Oscar, hugs him and makes a big show of kissing him on both cheeks.

OSCAR: What d'fuck are you doin'?

TOOT: I was watchin' a TV documentary there. That's what the French do. When you're leavin', they kiss y'on both cheeks.

OSCAR: I'm not fuckin' French.

TOOT: Only tryin' t'be nice, Oscar, get a grip.

DOMINIC enters.

DOMINIC: Hey Oscar, I'm glad I caught ya. Somebody says you have stuff for constipation? *(The others laugh.)* What the fuck are yous laughing at?

OSCAR: I have the very best of gear right here.

OSCAR takes a small box out of his pocket. Before he can do anything, DOMINIC snatches it out of his hands and moves off.

DOMINIC: Ah great, Oscar, thanks.

OSCAR: Hey, what da… Are y'not gonna wish me well?

DOMINIC speaks without looking at OSCAR or breaking stride as he exits.

DOMINIC: Am I fuck. You were never nice to me so why should I be nice to you. Cunt.

OSCAR is left dumbfounded. FREDDIE re-enters.

FREDDIE: C'mon Oscar, let's get a move on or the Governor might change his mind.

OSCAR: Okay.

He looks the two others up and down, thumps his heart passionately with his fist and hurries off.

See yiz.

HANK enters at stage left to face THUMPER entering at stage right.

THUMPER: So you finally got your release papers.

HANK: Yep. In fifteen minutes, I'll be flyin' up that M1 with the wind tearin' through m'hair.

THUMPER: You've been a good mate all these years.

HANK: We've had some good laughs. *(Beat.)* What about you? Where you gonna stay now that your grandmother's passed away?

THUMPER: Gonna try Dannielle. Y'know the daughter I had to Juicy Lucy? She lives out in Bangor.

HANK: You can crash with me if y'want. Until you get somewhere, like.

THUMPER looks into the distance pensively wondering where the hell he is going to live. He turns and gives HANK a forced smile.

THUMPER: No, I'll be alright.

HANK and THUMPER look at each other for a moment, then hug. HANK exits.

FREDDIE: 1984 was the year things hit rock bottom for me. The drinking had begun to catch up on me, when by chance, I read a phrase in the bible that said, 'Blessed are they that are persecuted in my name, for theirs is the kingdom of God.' From that moment onwards I never touched another drop of drink.

EAMON and TOOT are dancing and singing. Simultaneously, at the other end of the stage HANK and THUMPER are doing a funny walk in unison, whilst also singing.

EAMON, TOOT, HANK & THUMPER:
'Show me the way to go home
I'm tired and I wanna go to bed
I had a wee drink about an hour ago
And it's goin' right to my head...'

TOOT waves and says his goodbyes then jumps into a mini-bus. HANK does the same and gets into the same minibus.

PRISON OFFICER: Mini bus is leaving.

TOOT: See yiz, lads.

HANK: Good Luck!

TOOT: You for release too?

HANK: Yep. Seventeen of my best years – gone – left lingering *(Pointing.)* just over there somewhere.

TOOT: Me too. Eleven years and two weeks.

HANK: And this is the first time I've ever set eyes on you.

TOOT: My name's Toot. Toot McGinley, a Bealfeirstian from the Whiterock Road.

The two men shake hands.

HANK: Hank McNeely, Shankill Road. *(Beat.)* What's a Bealfeirstian...?

TOOT: Well you have Londoners and Glaswegians...

FREDDIE moves downstage.

FREDDIE: Nearly nine years now since the oul place closed down. I often wonder where they all are now Hank Toot Oscar and the others. I had a weird dream last night. A bloody weird dream.

The men immediately fall in to a military formation with OSCAR barking out the orders. They come to a halt and OSCAR steps forward.

OSCAR: Moved to Limerick with a woman I met at the All Ireland Fleadh in Donegal. Run a Spar shop and take fuck all d'do with fuck all. No Damian. *(Sings 'Tears Of A Clown' but song quickly fades.)*

OSCAR moves back into the formation and they resume marking time for a few seconds before stopping again. EAMON steps forward. (This same process is repeated until all have spoken.)

EAMON: Full-time elected politician now. I'm more often in Stormont than I am in m'own house. Cathy is happy as a pig in shit. She's in the party now too. *(Sings 'All My Loving'.)*

HANK: It's Community work for me. Happily married to Theresa-the-commie and we've two lovely kids. I lecture at The University Of Ulster one day a week. *(Sings Bob Dylan's 'Jokerman'.)*

THUMPER: Started with booze and ended with cocaine. Never leave the house now. I live with Danielle – the daughter I had d'Juicy Lucy – she's always on to me to wash. *(Sings 'You Really Got Me'.)*

OSCAR: Companyyyy, halt! Right turn! By the leftttt, quick march!

The men march off, leaving FREDDIE onstage.

FREDDIE: There it is. The story of ceis fada – the Long Meadow. The love of my life, Maureen has been dead two years now – cancer. Every day is...empty now. The daughter Ruth lives in France and wants me to move over there. I just might.

Off-stage, we hear a quick blast of loud marching feet.

FREDDIE: Oh. Almost forgot about one man.

TOOT comes running onstage and stops centre-stage.

TOOT: Fuck...you do not wanna hear about my life.

BLACKOUT

www.ingramcontent.com/pod-product-compliance
Ingram Content Group UK Ltd.
Pitfield, Milton Keynes, MK11 3LW, UK
UKHW020725280225
455688UK00012B/518

9 781849 430005